$$\&\text{\Large B52}$$

Thank you for Being
Such an AMAZING
AMBASSADOR for
the Ancestors and
the ARTS

Love Always,

Venus Jones

APCA
3-11-17

Lyrics for Langston

Venus Jones

Venus Jones

"Lyrics for Langston"

Poems by Venus Jones
Edited by Clarissa LeVonne Bolding and Resa Fromby
Resources and references provided by Rosalind Bartlett
Hug Support from Stephen Jones
Book Layout by Venus Jones
Front Cover Design by Ricc Rollins
Front Cover Photo by Bryan Leighty
Antique and Studio Assistance by Corinne Broskett and Venue Theatre

Please contact:
Venusian Publishing
bookings@venusjones.com
www.venusjones.com

Also by Venus Jones:
(available at VenusJones.com, CDBaby.com, or Amazon.com)

Venus to Earth (A trip around the word)
Polly-Ticks
Kwanzaa: 7 Days, 7 Principles (poems and affirmations for everyday living
She Rose (on a journey from girl to Goddess)

The following poems have been printed or recorded elsewhere:

"Chasing Freedom" appeared in *Liberated Muse: How I freed my soul* 2009.
"Dixie Land" appeared in the *St. Petersburg Times* 2002
        and in *She Rose* 2006.
"Swing Jazz Cats" appeared in *She Rose* 2006.

TABLE OF CONTENTS

~MOVEMENT~

EPILOGUE

~FOREWORD~

"History is the window to the future."

My grandmother Josephine always said, "Progress only comes if you are willing to make changes." After an hour of conversation, I knew that Venus Jones was the change I needed in order to move forward with the Langton Hughes Family Museum. This young woman also made me see that things can always be better, if you are willing to accept advice and suggestions from others. We as a people must be ready and able to accept the history of those who have gone before us. We say that we want change but lasting change only comes if we unite and work together. We must understand that History is the Window to the Future.

My first encounter with Venus Jones was quite by accident. One evening I was planning for my next exhibition and presentation of the Langston Hughes Family Museum and my phone rang. A polite voice said, "Hi I'm Venus Jones, I found you on the Internet. I'm seeking the rights to use an image of your cousin, Langston Hughes, for the cover of my book and I'd really like your permission." As our conversation progressed, it seemed as though we had an instant connection.

Both Langston Hughes and Venus Jones understand the importance of; Values, Legacy, History and Ancestors. They write about our people, - he in his time and she in the present. Her style and phrasing is so much like my cousin Langston, that it is almost scary! Some of her pieces I had to read more than once, just to make sure they came from the pen of Venus Jones and not that of Langston (Hughes). These two geniuses of the written and spoken word seem to have a lot in common. He has been her muse and her work reflects and channels his greatness. She is Langston Hughes in the form of a Black girl.

There are many of his poems that I read over and over like, "I'm Still Here," "Mother to Son," which I've shared with my son and "Weary Blues." But when I want to laugh I read "Madam to You," a collection of verse, about Alberta K. Johnson that lets you see that Madam had quite a history herself. The character Madam has already been done but Venus may create another character we can follow through life.

When I reflect on the person I knew as my cousin, and not THE Langston Hughes, Poet, Author and Playwright, I'm glad that I had the opportunity to know him as a family member. I look forward to knowing the Poet and Author Venus Jones better. But more importantly, I would love to have the opportunity to know her as a friend. May she continue to write and add to the great Tampa Renaissance and beyond, telling the world about our people and celebrating the people of her time. She is phenomenal and her work will speak for her. The world remembers Langston Hughes and the world will know and remember Venus Jones.

All Aboard! "People Get Ready, there's a train ah coming, don't need no baggage, just get on board." Ride along and take in the insightful work of Venus Jones!

Marjol Rush-Collet,
"Keeper of the Dream"
Langston Hughes Family Museum, Inc.

~ACKNOWLEDGEMENTS~

I am grateful for my dream developers and my dream destroyers, as they have provided the sunshine and the rain for my growth.

You know who you are.

x

~MUSIC~

"Blues has the pulse beat of a people who keep on going."

- Langston Hughes

DIXIE LAND

I've been weary.
I was black misery, full of red passion, but blue
walking blue

Then I heard this sound, and it's so true.
That horn had a familiar toot.
Sent sensations to the base of my roots.

It was a cool flute!
Had cats dressed in zoot suits,
doing the jitterbug while waiting in line!

So I stopped,
asked for directions, to the space and place,
where I could spend my dime.

No longer on the outside looking in.
I'm no stranger!
I'm what you call friend!

With my ten cents in hand, she says, "Thanks for coming!"
"Welcome to Dixie Land!"
  The bridge begins.

2

Packed in at 9:05!
All night...live!

He flips his suspenders, anticipating the play.
I could watch him do that solo grind every day!
He made that bell speak.

Someone hollered, "Talk to me! Preach!"
Then he'd do that hip walk
that made all the girls weak!

Bass had braids, trumpet had a fro,
but the sax man was bright, he 'phoned with a glow.
He blew my mind cool, as silver riffs rippled on the cymbal.

Ahhhhh... the chimes!
And there was nothing like a shot of rim from my Buddy Rich!
He turned into the *boom-clack* at the end of every line.
Boom-clack, like that!
He did it again.

Then the piano man began to tip-toe his fingers along my heart.
The midnight blues set starts.
His voice echoed through that smoky room.
A soulful melody met my flame.

I could taste eternal love;
I released all guilt and shame.
The dark cornea of my right eye became misty.

My aching heart bled light.
Colorful keys took me to a place up the scales,
as he tended the torn with tales of deliverance.

Caramel fingers tracing ivory milk,
and I tapped, tapped out of the hell that society built.
And baby... it was grand!

Just then, the lead vocalist rose from his bench,
strolled to the center of the band
with a black hat in his hand.
He threw it in the air, spun around and
caught it, on the tip of his spit-shined shoe!
Boom-clack!

The drum did a soft roll, as silence took its toll,
giving way to a thunderous and gracious crowd.
Oh, we hooted a constellation of praises, loud!

Do you know what they did?
They bowed!

SWING JAZZ CATS

The Crusaders charged in with the herd
when the crowd began to stray.
They said, "We're 'Picking up the Pieces'
the average big bands left yesterday."

This time, we wanted to do something
more than a simple side sway.
So we made some naughty noise!

And the girls started bouncing like baby boys
because that beat was jumpin'.
I mean really jumpin'!
Flipping and twisting them girls like toys!

Me? No, I Ain't Misbehavin!
But 'Out of the Blue,' Daddy-O had left.
"And what it is, cat?"
Lady Scat taking us back.
She said,

> *"It don't mean a thing, if it ain't got that swing!*
> *Doo Wop / Doo Wop / Doo Wop!*
> *Doo Wop / Doo Wop/ Doo Wop!*

It don't mean a thing, all you got to do is sing!
Doo Wop / Doo Wop / Doo Wop!
Doo Wop / Doo Wop / Doo Wop!

It makes no difference if it's sweet or hot!
Just give that rhythm everything you got!
Bada da Boo Bot Bot / Skeeda Doo Bot / A Doo Wat Wop!"

Whoa!
Ella was so full, she blew up the spot!
And Ooh Sha Bam, 'Bean-a-Re-Bop' Ka-Zam!
That joint was hot and heavy!
Grooving on a highway for Miles and Freddy.

Frankie knows it was a Maze of movement.
Thighs... Heels... Every toe tapping!

And I always meant to say,
"I got a kick out of you!"
And she? She would say,
"Baby... love is here to stay. You be sweet!"

I guess it just means there will always be spring in my feet.
I decided to get on up, so I could get on down!
Because these weary blues will never, ever, make me lose my beat!

METER AND RHYME

Some words live   to touch and agree

Some poems have a lock

They also have a key

         When verse is swinging

High

      and

            Low

it sounds like call and response

               A harmonic flow

RETROGRADE

Let's go back,

"Back Down Memory Lane."

Like George Jefferson, we strutted in the place!

Everywhere we turned was a smiling face.

We didn't let the world dictate our state!

We decided to unwind, with nothing but unity on the mind.

We chanted, *"These…are…the…good…times!"*

Then we jumped in those soul train lines.

"Can you dig it?

I do mean, "Super Fly! Groovy! Right on!"

We chanted in song.

Somebody said,

"Is it that Foxy Brown or Cleopatra Jones?"

Watch out now! I'm *"On my own."*

Making you rewind to Mr. Rerun,

Back to bell-bottoms and big fun,

That floppy denim hat!

Wait a minute! Afro is where it's at!

Like a Panther, ready to give power back to the people
and if need be, protect your family from some dirty feds.

Casually speaking, we were rocking Pro-Keds,
sporting the tie dye, polyester, ponchos,
pom-poms and platform boots.

Don't forget those wheels, that made everyone want to
"Toot, Toot! Ahhh... Beep, Beep! Toot, Toot! Ahhh... Beep, Beep!"
Who's that rolling in the blue beetle down the street?

We were saying it loud! We were just as proud!
Making America march to a black is beautiful beat.
Because we needed those hits, *"Good God!"*

That's what made us move our feet and
"We liked it, uh-huh, uh-huh!"
Then it was, *"Bounce... Rock... Skate...Roll"*
We had so much soul!

They had to slide us some more bread my man!
Because we built some businesses more "solid"
than a brick house on land!

When we did the twist, the jerk, the shotgun, the swim.

Then along came a snake.

So we were Running Man, to the Cabbage Patch.

Had to Lock and Pop into a Break.

Got fixed at the hip on the flipside.

We asked that you sit back and enjoy this Hip-Hop ride.

The mission was to stay smooth, I do mean like butter!

Because the money was so brand new,

it was "fresh and clean."

When things got hot,

we started chilling on the down low…

You know what I mean…

don't always need to be seen.

Some of us were out of sight and out of mind.

Started chanting stuff like "I'm bad," two times!

And when we were bad, we took all that was good

to an old and new school.

Because we were still, "Dy-no-mite!"

So much that we became "The Bomb!"

We were so fine and sharp, we stayed on point.

Do you realize that we rocked every funky joint?
And every time we decide to fly *"Up, up to the sky,"*
what we create tends to multiply.
Sometimes we spread the truth
and sometimes, in stereo, we spread the typical lie.

Let us be cautious,
not fall slave to the system and slang.
But on what stem does that turning leaf hang?

Somebody say, "Word!"
Because it is the word, the style, and rhythm
that we help maintain.

I'm your Soular Sister signing off.
So what's up, black?
Gimmie some love, don't hate!

Cut me some slack
and if you're "Ready or not…"
It's time we all get back.

"Back to life, back to reality…
Back to the here and now.
Oh, yeah!"

THE STATE OF HIP

Some believed we'd find a better fate,
if and when we chose to integrate.
Well a desire for roots or rebellion,
from the illusion followed that state.

So his way of life is to take a life.
He said, "We only have one life to live."
Some pour out libation for the deceased dead,
like it's all we got to give.

The day that the Tupac died,
I began writing this poem,
not knowing my desire,
for sacred music
would last this long.

Remember when there were real emcees,
that made us proud?
When the DJ played,
there wasn't a need to
pump up the crowd.

Original art was sprayed,
B-boys and B-girls had to take a break!
Where has real Hip-Hop gone?
I haven't seen her as of late.

Only a few think critically, supporting whatever
comes into the cipher.
Most invest in whatever images
MTV claims are nicer.

So the underground became mainstream
when gangster rap was born.
It's just like Hollywood now,
the restless and the torn.

He said, "This is something we can take
on a global marketing ride!
Who needs songs about black love
and who cares about black pride?"

We were headed for self-destruction.
We knew it was out of our hands.
We were clueless when Flava asked,
about the time, over and over again.

Some fell in love with the hype,

while others bought it too,

What else was there to do?

Violence and sex sells, this is true.

They auctioned off Rock-n-Roll,

He lost his natural soul and

I use to love Hip-Hop but

Now she's out of control.

I guess it doesn't matter,

If you have to drop it every night.

He plays, "Get Low";

you smile, like it's alright.

Yet too many talk harmonious jazz

on stage in the poetry scene.

Then change tune; disrespecting each other,

when in search of power and bling.

Question is: Who's running it?

Let us divide again.

Do you know where that message came from?

Not you my friend?

Are we still on the same team, like black king, black queen?
Who produced a tight track
and piled on crap to make green?

That booming bass surrounds me,
as I backslide and slip.
Now you know they put some juju on it,
I almost lost my grip!

I don't even like this song,
but I'm found dancing on the floor.
But I still want something even better
than we had before.

So you also see me standing by
and sometimes standing alone.
I have to find a new station
and good music on my own.

Some friends are nodding,
like they never heard me scream or shout.
One day they'll understand
and I won't have to go another bout.

One day, more artists will use their gifts

to make the blind see.

Until then, I'm promoting balance.

Holla if you hear me!

I AM TELLING YOU!

And I am telling you, I am going!

You're the worst man I've ever known!

Take your hands off me, I'm grown!

There's no no no no…way!

I'm staying here with you.

I'm not staying here with you!

Because I want to live free.

I'm leaving!

I'm leaving!

And you can't control me!

I'VE BEEN 'BUKED

I've been the bottomless pit of despair,
In search of a band-aid; a drug.

I've been the one in hope of repair,
The lowered head; the shrug.

I've had eyes glazed over dead.
I've been the broken and torn.

I've had heavy feet of lead.
I've been 'buked and scorned.

ORIGINAL

He is a bold impression,
full of contrasting colors,
that shimmer through cracked glass.

Hear him open up; so young.
Happy a big break came fast.
Watch him open up and become empty,
only to suffer with the shard at night.

He's a soulful song, fading, fading,
fading from sight!
They say his mindful masterpiece
was good, but now it's simply old.
And another random artist
grows pale, trembling, cold.

He's moonlighting on the corner.
Holding out a cup...
A howling has been! How?
How? How did original dry up?

19

~WORDS~

"I don't need my freedom when I'm dead.
I cannot live on tomorrow's bread."

- Langston Hughes

HEALING WORDS

"Take a stab at it!"
"You'll knock 'em dead!"
"Break a leg," that's what they said.
They told me I would "make a killing" on stage.
They said I just had to "bring the pain and rage."

I needed a good "push" or some great "plan of attack."
I was sure to "blow up," if I could get a "kick back."
They told me when distress came to "conquer my fears."
Who has time to sit with the truth? I'm "fighting tears."

When we live for "the struggle," we "build up walls."
We find it funny to "burst her bubble" or "bust his balls."
They said the best way is to always "beat the competition!"
"Cut out the middle man!"
"Arm yourself with ammunition!"

Is life about "choosing battles" on this bloody field?
Or am I "blocking a blessing" with a cold hard shield?
They told me, "Kill two birds with just one stone!"
(versus "Set two birds free at once, to soar on their own.")

She said, "I really enjoy picking your brain!"
Am I the *only* one who thinks this sounds insane?

We have a war on poverty, terrorism, and drugs.
Is a war on war speech the answer?
I see blank faces and shrugs.

Would it begin by me saying
that I'd prefer to be at peace with you?
We won't always agree,
but sharing our intention is the thing to do.

If someone says that's not true,
ask them why they feel a specific way.
You may find it's not just black and white;
it's shades of blue and gray.

If you're giving old words new meanings
and your ideas keep getting "shot down,"
Imagine words that unite people,
giving off a higher vibration at the sound.

If you say your anti anything,
it only adds fuel to fire in debate.
I monitor my own thoughts
and still fall into the slang of hate.

But if words are symbols and
these phrases; symptoms and signs,
May we create loving expressions that
open hearts and mend minds?

BREAD

I come to get fed.
Poetry is bread.

Give me honey wheat or white!
I'll never dread.
Poetry is bread.

Sweet banana and corn bread, all over my plate,
I come early, don't ever want too be late!
I come to get fed buttermilk biscuits.

Did ya hear what I said?
Italian, pumpernickel,
I can get full off of flat or rye!
I ain't fickle!

I'm hungry…
Feed me Seymour, Hillary, Shante, and Fred!

Poetry is bread.
It fills up my soul.
It nourishes my head.

Jesus Christ broke poetry,

Before He rose from the dead.

So break me off a piece of that pita!

Share multi-grains of pain before you tread.

If this was the last supper,

tell me about the path you've led.

I come to get fed.

No margarine, butter instead.

Poetry is wholesome and holy

Bread.

ODE TO SIDE SALADS

Lyrics have lined my lips.
Munched on metaphors and
Similes have been sipped.

Ate alliteration just the other day.
"Well, I was chewing on couplets and characters
while devouring dialogue," so she say.

I told her I could get full off a little subplot.
"Not I! Pass me a symbol while this stanza is hot!"

All this assonance is also
arousing to my appetite.
But it shows on my hips,
so I'm on that diction tonight.

She's fiction to butter up bread,
for these satirical ballads.
The irony of her palette,
sparked my ode to side salads.

THE ZOUND OF ZORA

I'm salsa, sitting next to brown rice, screaming,
"I'm the perfect side!"
As courageous as collard greens,
making the clergy tongue-tied.

Have you ever seen sweet potatoes,
sashaying down a dusty road?
C'mon and walk with me, into the horizon.
Honey there's a journey to behold!

A fixin' of tall tales and short stories
That'll save a country-fried soul.
A Cajun woman, who can mix
with biscuits, like Mr. Big, butter, roll.

Some lemon-lime and pear wine
Lingers on these licorice lips.
Jonah's Gourd vine got wrapped up,
All around these curvaceous hips.

With a caramel camera in one hand,
Pen and paper in my stylish sack.
I'm flirting with the moon, the swamp,
catfish, and some gator outback.

I carry a gilded six-bit, ever since
I stole the keys to all the locks.
Shoot! Because I'm a hot spring,
You can pour me out on the coldest rocks.

And ain't no hoo doo in America ever
got a spell that's stronger than me.
Queen of the baracoon cause
Oshun knows my rhythm echoes the sea.

I love myself when I'm laughing, and
when I'm mean, I'm still divine.
I'm Zora Neale Hurston and,
like the Suwannee River,
I'm rough and refined.

SLIM PICKENS MEETS A FASHION COP

Some fashion cop came around
and wanted my name to put it down.

I said, "Slim Pickens!"
He snickered, "I can see."
I said...

"Yo I'm styling! Ask Honey Bee!
They call me Slim cause I'm slim and
Pickens cause I'm smart.
You think I'm out of touch
but what I wear is art.

"I stay suited in silk
for the red carpet affair
That's why I got this pimp cane.
She keeps these braids in my hair.

"This green straw hat;
I got it a while back
at the player's ball;
out' Nelly's Cadillac!

"This knee length shirt
is an extra perk.
The Scarface print
makes 'em go berserk."

He said, "But why you in a leather jacket?
It's eighty degrees!"

I said, "Yo man, whatever…
I'm cool as a breeze."

TOO DAMN LONG!

The man that knows something
knows he knows nothing at all.
I guess you've never heard that verse,
so we're at a slow crawl.

You're not the only one on the list,
other folk can tell and show!
The host must be on crack;
I mean really, where did he go?

Look! Do you even care,
if the audience is dead or alive?
It wouldn't be so bad,
but you talk a whole lot of jive!

I swear you've been on the stage
since a quarter past eight!
How long is your poem?
I mean it's getting ugly late!

It's almost midnight and

I hate that we've come so far!

Man, why can't you save mic hogging,

for the featured star?

A half an hour ago,

I was feeling your groove,

so don't get me wrong!

But that was before I realized,

your poem was just

too... damn... long!

ACTING A FOOL

My heart could be breaking.
My head could be aching.
So often, I get my feelings hurt.
All I have to do is sit next to you,
I'll be laughing at all the dirt!

It really doesn't matter the place,
my friend, you don't care if it's a crime.
No one has a more castigating face,
when they're asked to share a dime.

We could be in Sunday school,
in the front row, listening to a sanctified sermon.
I can't turn your way at all when the usher comes,
Cause I know that you're determined.

To make me laugh so hard, I lose control,
and there goes my natural mind.
I start rolling out of my seat, like it's the goal.
Acting a fool, having a hell of a time!

WHAT MY GRANDMOTHER TOLD ME

Your mouth gon' write a check your behind can't cash!
I think it's best you find a J.O.B. real fast.
Because right now, you talk a lot bigger than your money stash.
Your mouth gon' write a check your behind can't cash.

Why do you have to have the last word there honey?
I'm the boss of you and ain't a damn thing funny!
You have your own mind and that's real cool.
Now earn your own roof, if you want new rules.

You still have my milk on your breath and I can see.
that you have a long way to your Ph.D.

Your mouth gon' write a check your behind can't cash!
I think it's best you find a J.O.B. real fast.
Because right now, you talk a lot bigger, than your money stash.
Your mouth gon' write a check your behind can't cash.

EVERYTHING MUST CHANGE

Change.

Do you have some?

Change.

I'm just trying to make a dollar out of fifteen.
Wow. You read my mind!

Put LIFE IS ABOUT CHANGE on your sign.

Whatchu talkin' bout fool? I ain't no bum!

Well change your clothes and stop with the gimme some.
Are you afraid of a big change?

Man I just wanted a broken down dollar!

Yeah! I just wanted to add my two cents.

Nice of you! But don't bother!

Change!

Man, I'm about to catch a case!

Change!

Man, you better get out of my face!

PULL OVER

When the siren goes off, I slowly pull over
into Wal-Mart's parking lot.
My heart is beating so fast and
I feel like my stomach is in a knot.

I can only focus on the lights, flashing red and white.
Thinking is he going to beat me blue, or read me my rights.
I'm dead with no attorney and, No, I'm not wanted by the feds,
but in these parts, I hear they like to collect Negroes' heads!

He steps out of the car when two other patrolmen join the scene.
I start sweating bullets, hoping this is a bad dream.

He bangs on the back of my trunk
unlike an officer, who promotes peace.
I remember how to make my disdain
for crooked cops cease.

So I say, "Is there a problem officer?
I want to calm any nerves.
I apologize for any wrong doing and
know you're here to protect and serve."

"License and registration,"
he says with a penetrating stare.
"Did you know you didn't use your signal,
changing lanes back there?"

I'm thinking, I didn't realize not using a signal
was such an excessive crime.
It takes three police cars to remind me,
or to put me back in line?

I said, that's what I was thinking;
I actually was careful with my tongue.
"I was following a friend, sir, and forgot.
How could I be so dumb?"

Then I just sat quietly, waiting patiently,
in hopes to be released,
and gave thanks to God for humor
and for giving me nice teeth.

He said I was free to go,
I knew some time had past.
I said, "It won't happen again, sir."
Then they sped off really fast.

First, I reflected on the word "free,"
before I decided to go.
Thinking, whoever they thought I was
escaped fifteen minutes ago.

WAS HE BLACK?

(Written on September 11, 2002)

A young man flew his plane into Tampa's Bank of America.
Was he a terrorist?
You ask, "Was he black?"

When a young man put pipe bombs in mailboxes,
Was he a terrorist?
You ask, "Was he black?"

When a young man went on a journey
and joined Al Qaeda, spoke a new tongue,
Was he a terrorist?
You ask, "Was he black?"

If I said he was black,
would you say, "I figured that?"
If I said he was brown, would you say,
"He helped bring the twin towers down?"

But if I said he was white,
would you say, "Hmm, that's not right?"
"He must have been temporarily insane."
"Was he on medication?"

"He must have gotten on the wrong track."
"Now how can we get that young man back?"

If he were brown or black, would you have said that?
Would his medication been an unknown or insignificant fact?

Because the war on terrorism didn't start with Timothy McVeigh,
Nor did it begin on 9/11, a year ago today.
Some believe it started when Columbus
stumbled on the red man and broke the pact.

Some say it started when 110,000 Asians were detained
during the very first "Whites-Are-The-Only-Patriots Act."

Today, over 5,000 Arabs rot in jail cells,
guilty by skin color association.
Christianity is the only right faith
in this due process of elimination.

So sit quiet, pray, and have faith in the system,
all ye of darker hue.
But please don't hold your breath,
because poetic justice is truly overdue.

When it comes to the war on blacks,

I just want to go 39 years back.

That's when North America

lost all of her taste and tact.

Sunday, September 15, 1963,

I hope you'll never forget.

A tender 11 and 14 died on 9/15,

in the 16th Street Baptist.

On 9/15 the building was a progressive

and freedom-fighting church,

where four little girls were found dead.

She's dressed in her Sunday best,

with blood, concrete, and glass spilling from her swollen head.

This bombing was different;

the spirit of the civil rights fight, they sought to kill.

Even a racist southern belle suggested

that the murder of a female child was ill.

We lost more than one precious and rare pearl.

The rest of the world, mourned the stolen promise

of each bright, brown-skinned and freshly cut girl.

But in the divided states,

victims and terrorists lived side by side.

Criminals roamed in circles, with torches,

in search of a sturdy tree.

And it's a proven fact that J. Edgar Hoover,

the FBI, and the Klan,

were all working together to some degree...

to stop liberation.

To stop liberation!

    To stop liberation!

      To stop movement!

      To silence the wanna-be

voting, well-versed, brief case toting,

financially and mentally free.

The penalty was extreme, only if you looked brown or black.

Unfortunately, I have to add a drop of pigmentation, see?

Final convictions may have never been made

if it wasn't for Spike Lee digging up dirt from the grave.

The grieving families buried their own,
and cried alone in a separate community.
The nation didn't unite against terror,
wave flags, or sing songs in unity.

This poem is for:
>   Cynthia Wesley,

>   Carole Robertson,

>   Addie Mae Collins

>   and

>   Denise McNair.

Some Americans have forgotten about the day the children died,
with midnight eyes and bushy hair.

Like the 250 million lost in the Middle Passage,
the countless castrated and raped,
injected with syphilis, dragged, and beat,
the 600 black-owned businesses,
bombed from the air in Tulsa, on Black Wall Street,

The tortured, lynched, murdered.

The bred and sold, who slaved.

This kind of terrorism has had a long existence

in the home of the brave.

For over 400 years, terrorists led scavengers

in a variety of systematic packs.

Thanks to Jim Crow's policy, white sheets just took

what they lacked, like sneaky racing rats.

Today you may find a poor black cat chasing his own skinny tail.

He's in prison, probation, parole, or in jail.

There are some strays that dash across the finish line without fail

with arms stretched out to the sky,

giving thanks for the way they got over,

like those black men in white movies who aren't the first to die.

After a long jump, a million marches,

and a wall of ebony and ivory grins,

did you know that in 1995,

not one but over 40 black churches burned again?

Do the people always have to loot,
or stoop as low as the oppressor to make amends?
Will all impoverished people of color
catch up to that Euro dollar trend?

America could repay the descendents of her enslaved with:

    affordable healthcare,

    a quality education,

    decent housing and

        at least one

          profitable opportunity.

But until then, just try to pretend O.J. didn't need
at least 40 acres and one loyal mule to win.

The liberty lady who weighs these facts
is actually a blind old bat.
She just learned to sniff all along that money track.
Will you forget the numbers?

Will you forget how survivors of ethnic profiling
and economic terrorism chose to react?
And the next time they speak of a terrorist,
will you ask, "Was he black?"

FATHER FIGURES

To my big brother
who cooked up a hot meal
He was top chef
on that Foreman Grill

To my uncle
who talked a whole lot of smack
To grandpa
who showed us how to give back

To my favorite male teacher,
coach, and monk
We called him Daddy–O
he taught us jazz and funk

To my cousin
who helped us through the pain
Not biological but just
like a father I claim

BLACKER THAN THOU

I just wanna be black.
I wanna be blacker than black.
I was teased for the pigment I lack.
Now, I'm that pot in the back.
I'm calling out the kettle,
with a flame to settle, color struck to my core,
"Don't call me white no more!"

I just wanna be black.
Not yellow, red, or pecan brown.
I'm black, the coolest color around.
I'm no pretty boy with a loose curl!
I'm rejecting my daddy's swirl.
I'm black.

So black, I become blue.
Now I can only talk about slavery.
Now I can only talk about a coup.
Because I'm blacker than black.
I'm blacker than you;
I'm tried and true to my African race.
You can see some serious black, all over my face.

I scream the word "Revolution!" ten times a day.

I wear dashikis and "Free Africa," you'll hear me say.

I'm still posing for each picture,

with a raised arm and clinched fist.

I am "Soul on Ice,"

listening to "Guerillas in the Mist."

Sometimes, I gather up all the dark-skin blacks I can find.

Hoping they don't notice I'm lighter than their kind.

In a bullhorn, "All you do-good Oreos and crackers stay clear!"

Shhhh, I make a whole lot of money off this platform of fear.

To the camera, "I'm a target, because I unite blacks down here."

Between you and me,

I refuse to talk to black gays.

I don't speak Arabic or Spanish.

Hell no to Creoles!

I measure blackness by region, class,

and the media's opinion polls.

No breakfast programs for your little panther,

No counsel for the weak, before the cops patrol.

No plan, no point, no prevention...

I sold my soul.

Funny thing is, I live in a big white house,

in the suburbs, on Shady Oaks Drive.

And they say I only pop up

when there's heat, like corn, to talk jive.

Such a national security threat to the establishment,

they keep my black ass alive!

~LOVE~

*"Folks, I'm telling you, birthing is hard and dying is mean —
so get yourself a little loving in between."*

- Langston Hughes

WHAT YOU ARE TO ME

I want to kiss you when you're dreaming,
slip into your subconscious sanctuary.

Sometimes I listen to your heartbeat at night,
cuddling closer to match the sound.

I wish I could number each strand of hair on your head.
Like Jesus, jealous that God knows you better.

You're in mid-sentence sometimes when I start smiling,
and it's funny, because it's not what you said!

I'm smiling at who you are,
because I love who you are.
I love what you are to me.

HE'S WATCHING OVER ME

I found him,

that man I dreamt of,

and now we're the picture of love.

He's watching over me...

So much I need some space.

Can someone tell him to get out of my face?

I can't rest or barely pee!

I love this man.

But I also love privacy!

PILL FOR THE PAIN

If there's never going to be peace in the Middle East,
may I find peace in the middle of your arms?

If there's never going to be universal healthcare,
may I find wellness in a bucket of your charms?

If the ozone layer continues to tear
and Mother Earth decides to die.
May I give you a final kiss, my friend,
as my last hurrah and goodbye?

"Carpe diem,"
    "que sera sera,"
        "no day but today,"
          "so it is,"
            "let it be."
If there's a quake, an attack, a tornado,
a race war, or another tsunami.

If we'll always be in love forever,
roaming free from a horrid hurricane,
may we escape, only to create our own drama?
May we be each other's pill for the pain?

SILLY LOVE SONGS

When we're together, even on the phone,
I find myself singing silly love songs.

A jingle about chores you did on your own,
I find myself singing silly love songs.

A master of sappy verse when in the zone,
I find myself singing silly love songs.

A tune about the sweet poot you've blown,
I find myself singing silly love songs.

You move me to chorus even when alone,
I find myself singing silly love songs.

THE ART OF ONENESS

We can hold hands and be filled with deep emotion.

This thought makes me reminisce

and smile at the rushing waves ahead.

Now tears of gratitude flood my eyes.

I refuse to look at you, in this moment,

given you're reading more than words.

So I sit still, in silence,

as the young flaunt their flings.

On this beach full of bohemians,

I level the sand beneath my feet.

And wonder what they really know

about lasting love.

About the sacred art of oneness.

MY BROTHER FOR KEEPS

I find comfort in his presence,
like a tree he's my shade.
Rare and willing to clean up
the mess other's made.

He rocks back and forth
just to see me smile.
Breaks into dance to remind me,
to play for a while.

If his energy is low,
his eyes still light up when we meet.
He knows he's creating a buzz,
with all that honey sweet.

Like a soldier,
he guards the grounds around his black seed.
So alert,
he passes on wine and the taste of green weed.

He's serious about his word,

his desire to be on one accord.

You start to hum like Mavis,

at the thought of his mental sword.

"Oooh child, things are going to get easier and brighter, right now."

He just picks up burdens with his humor

and we're lighter somehow.

"Color him father,"

he put in back breaking hours and treasured time.

"Color him love,"

he rolled up his sleeves and jumped in the longest line.

He is that cool black cat,

a symbol of the majestic and proud.

His moves are subtle,

as he unites people in every crowd.

The masons, mercenaries and missionaries

know his name.

He cracked the spine on the book,

studying rules of the game.

He walks into blocks and circles
that are foreign to some,
because he measures the words
that leave the tip of his tongue.

Very few judge him by his pigment or hue.
They're looking for his confident cue.

All those in his court earned support
and have a keen sense of direction.
Maintaining a position means diving deep
into one's soul for dissection.

A warrior priest, ready to listen and teach,
he's strategic in his fight.
He packs a coat of armor,
knowing a sunny day will give to cold night.

He's proving with a centered head,
two arms, and two legs, you can.
He is a father, a son, and part of that higher spirit
dwelling on land.

My brother's keeper, keep on!
Just keep on keeping on, black man!

THE AUTHORS FELL OUT

(Inspired by a note Langston Hughes wrote on a copy of the play Mule Bone)

The authors fell out,
I'm sorry to say.
I had a bone to pick,
on the grounds of our play.

I never stole the script,
seeking rights and extension.
I gave contribution,
she gave me contention.

She said I wrote nothing,
but she had a grudge, you see?
And once her fears got a hold,
she was as stubborn as can be.

So we split over the split
when the Depression hit.
Negro life ain't funny
when folks have a fit.

Who's really to blame?
Some say our patron.
God bless Zora,
but she was no matron!

Business is business,
I think you'll agree.
The authors fell out,
and it got ugly.

The authors fell out,
leaving each other's side.
I really forgave Zora.
Love's stronger than pride!

TAKE A PICTURE

(What I imagine Zora Neale Hurston would have said
about a photo snafu of an "ordinary black girl" in her likeness.)

Take a picture of an ordinary black girl
And I hope you'll see me
Smiling with ease
Laughing out loud
With a traditional
"Girl please!"

Hand on one hip
Head cocked to the side
Ashy elbows sometimes
Full of audacious pride
Take a picture of an ordinary black girl

Looking impressive and mean
Jumping some weathered rope
Looking fragile, climbing green
Poking and prying with a purpose
Before and after Sunday service

She's wishing she was like her mama
Sporting the perfect hat
She's reading her favorite book
On the porch swing out back
So take a picture of an ordinary black girl

On an ordinary day
Telling a story
In her very own
Beautiful way

Clapping
Prancing
Dipping and Dancing

Take a picture of her
Taking a picture
Just an ordinary black girl

And I hope you'll see her through
She may be a modern day Zora,
Just trying in every way
To be her extraordinary self
Just like you
Just like you

DEAR PRECIOUS

Dear Precious,

I was called "dumb, no good, lazy, a fool!"
These were her kind words after school.
My best advice: Girl, you stay hungry for the truth!
Let your higher education be 100% proof.

Yet and still, you can find me focusing on my faults;
still killing ANTS (Automatic Negative Thoughts).
But before it is over, I'll be that affirmation queen.
My imagination has already mended the torn seam.

And it can take some time to find this place
where I have inner peace and a sense of grace.
I pledge to take care of my precious self.
I will practice physical and spiritual health.

I'm saying it loud, "Breaker-Breaker, One and Nine!"
For all those ignoring predators and the sign.
Do you read me, or are you just looking for glory?
All because you're tired of this sad story.

Yet and still, the ill voice rings daily in her ears.
Yet and still, there's a little boy inheriting his father's fears.

Who among us will do the "greater works"
and restore the living dead?
"Each one, teach one," is the mantra of
prevention in my head.

It was Langston's mother who said,
"Life ain't no crystal stair!"
Especially for those who look in the mirror
and hate their skin and their hair,

Especially for the illiterate who don't know
their heritage is there, hidden in a book.
I know the A-B-C's and 1-2-3's of my victorious history,
and yes, I borrowed this look!

I will pass these fundamental proverbs
and passages on down,
until the bitter becomes sugar baby
and you claim your sweet crown.

Step by step, walk on into the future

beyond this abuse and neglect.

Where it is written, no one has to beg

for the food that they get.

Until then, a Sapphire knows I have a torch

that shines in the tunnels in the middle of Nowhere.

And if you love yourself,

Baby girl, you're there!

You're rare!

A glorious gem that pushed,

despite the pressure and the time.

And we will stand in awe at your beauty,

because you are... precious and DIVINE!

COPASETIC

When I was five, my first grade teacher knew
I was all-the-way live and energetic.
So when others napped, I assisted with snacks,
and it was completely copasetic.

When I was seven, they put me in a play
and I was a black pilgrim, smiling, unapologetic.
I was standing right next to a white Indian,
and it was completely copasetic.

Well when I was nine, I broke my left wrist
and my teacher seemed a little empathetic.
"The show must go on!"
See, I was Dorothy, and even though
I resembled someone with a prosthetic,
she said, "Pretend your arm got hurt in the twister!"
It looked completely copasetic!

In the sixth grade, I transferred to a new school
and I was instantly magnetic.
They wanted to fight over my friendship,
and I thought, "Now this is completely copasetic."

The seventh and eighth grades, I can't remember.
So they must've been pretty pathetic.

I do remember when puberty hit,
as I became synthetic.
You could find me stuffing my bra,
cause y'all know, fat tissue is not genetic!

I went to eleven schools as a kid!
Moving left an aftertaste, like the acetic.
Eventually I earned my college degree,
while mastering radio and TV, like the kinetic.

Moral of the story is:
Everything will meet your satisfaction,
if you choose to let it.

You begin to expect something good,
and no matter the challenge,
you never sweat it.

And that's when you know you're living life
like everything is everything,
and it will always be completely copasetic!

~MOVEMENT~

"We younger Negro artists now intend to express our individual dark-skinned selves, without fear or shame. If white people are pleased, we are glad. If they aren't, it doesn't matter. We know we are beautiful. And ugly too... If colored people are pleased, we are glad. If they are not, their displeasure doesn't matter either. We build our temples for tomorrow, as strong as we know how, and we stand on the top of the mountain, free within ourselves."

- Langston Hughes

CHASING FREEDOM

I remember being snatched from my mother's arms.
Her arms turned into black sand when I reached for her.
She held up her head and stood firm with her feet together.

Like a cross on the Ivory Coast,
then she transformed into foam on a cold and distant shore.
I dream she's still all together.
I dream she's more than a pile of dirt and water.

She's waiting for me, standing there, like the scales of justice.
Waiting for me to contact her in my own time.
It's past midnight and I'm still lost.
Searching for the way home.

Stripped nearly naked in the winter,
sobbing in a foreign tongue,
I'm banging on a wooden door, asking for help.
My back is aching, feet blistered now.

I feel abandoned by my family.
I feel abandoned by my God.
I feel my hope-strained heart beating in my neck now.
I feel like I'm running… after freedom.

RACE (The Tortoise and the Hare)

Someone yelled, "Race!"
And we started rushing.
I fell in a deep ditch and
had to crawl out on my own!

Several of us are still stuck
in those black booby traps.
I started to blame my team,
to ease the bunny's burden.

Because every turtle knows,
every group has a pit for the poor.
But the haughty hare ain't that swift.
He's trying to cover us all in dirt.

So he'll be the first to finish!
And too many sportsman are dying
in unmarked graves,
over colors, in this silly competition!

YES WE CAN!

They told me blacks couldn't play lead parts
with natural hair.
That was before Whoopi Goldberg
made locs cool to wear.

They told me black models
are at the bottom of the fashion scene.
That was before Tyra Banks
became the top beauty queen.

They told me blacks were not
allowed on the nicest golf course.
That was before Tiger Woods
got in the swing full force.

They told me tennis was for rich girls
with white poodles and blonde bobs.
That was before Venus and Serena
started slamming on grand snobs.

They told me blacks couldn't
make movies that everyone wanted to see.
That was before Spike Lee
made green with controversy.

They told me no black man will ever
be president of the US of A.
That was before Obama said, "Yes we can!"
The most patriotic thing to say!

IS BARACK THE BUTLER?

"Is Barack the butler?" she asked,
as he scurried at a graceful pace,
preparing plans for the party.

She was amazed he had grace.
"You call this civil service?"
She thought she had more class.

As he served a full course of food at the table,
she said, "I'll pass."
He smiled when she was rude.

She said, "I have a cold."
He offered her a white cloth.
She said, "I prefer the old."

He stood politely at attention.
To her, he stood idly by.

He's ready to clean the house.
She's so sick, she could die.

I TOO SING A NEW SONG

I used to cry at the mere sight of red white and blue.
Standing at attention with my hand over my heart.
Tears before the second note of the anthem could begin.
That "Oh, say can you see, by the dawn's early" part.

Can't recite the constitution, but I'm ready to fight.
I'm a Senior Petty Officer, proud and packing.
I had a strong grip on Old Glory in the color guard.
My flag was full of any confidence I was lacking.

In uniform, I heard my freedom flip and flap.
Eyes forward, with only white stars in sight.
I was really patriotic, chanting "We are number one!"
But the wind blew my pole too far right.

My grandfather was a Staff Sergeant in the Army.
He earned a purple heart getting shot twice.
But, dressed as a civilian, he wasn't respected.
Mother said he found work. They sufficed.

Told me he tossed and turned when he slept,

and he'd wake up screaming at times.

He served his country for five years and never complained.

I just pretended to serve mine.

R.O.T.C. is where I learned to say, "Yes, sir!"

A habit I've never outgrown.

Garfield High was no Korea,

but, to some kids, it was a war zone.

Wearing the wrong colors meant you might get lost.

We had to pick sides, or a group.

I chose the one with shiniest buckles and the cleanest suits.

But today, I've made peace with the poor.

I'm a world citizen, I claim.

My country may go to war for oil,

But it won't go in my name.

Now, I'll pledge allegiance to a merciful God first,

one that teaches us to protect the Earth

to which we all belong.

This allows me the sovereignty

to create a new nation

and, if need be, a new song.

WHITE AND RONG (WAR)

He said, "What are you?

Where you from?

Brooklyn? Queens? The Flats?"

I said, "It ain't where you from.

It's where you going?

or like Rakim said,

'Where ya at?'"

Since I knew a little Hip-Hop history,

He automatically assumed I was "black."

And began to push up on me,

So I had to break him down.

I said, "First, I have a man.

So wait a minute, don't clown!"

He said, "He let you run free?"

"I have a marriage of liberation, not incarceration.

I am where I want to be.

But if you look a little closer,

you'll see he's in another conversation,

standing beside me."

He said, "You couldn't find a black man?"

Yes! He was bold, with a clear goal.

I told him his good old boy Clarence Thomas

looks black, but has no soul.

"Listen, he thinks a lot like Bono from U2.

Let me introduce you."

He said, "Who?"

I said, "Is being black the only necessity for you?"

"Woman don't you know your history?"

I said, "I represent the mother of all civilization

This is no biological mystery.

I'm proud that I roll with a diverse crew.

Are there 36 colors, or three primary flavors?"

"I don't know!"

I said, "Hmmm…thought you knew,

when scientists can't even agree.

You see, I earned my college degree

and you too could benefit from a class in anthropology."

He said, "Whatever... you married the white man!"

I said, "I'm married **to** a white man

and he happens to be the right man.

Mr. Wrong was like, "Your loss, you could've had me!"
I was thinking, "Whoa! Woo! Controversy!"

"Stop right there!
I didn't even know you,
and given your rush to judgment,
I don't think you would've ever been in the running, boo.
When I was younger, I did my homework.
And someone that sounded a lot like you said I was 'acting white.'
When then and now, I continue to uplift this 'black' plight.

"So no, rude boy, I didn't rule out any colors in my Crayola box.
But funny thing is, I used to think
that white women who dated black men
should be put on lock.

"For years, I shook my head at the thought
of coloring outside the line,
Until Cupid shot an arrow straight through my behind!

"So at this point, you can date a white woman or
marry a white man and I'd be fine."

He sang, "*She got jungle fever. He got jungle fever...*"

"I know... it's all about the fever for the forbidden flavor,

because all mixed couples are the same.

All whites are rich and want blacks

physically or mentally chained.

"If you hate white people so much,

why are you wearing their clothes?

Why are you drinking their beer

and watching their TV shows?

"Acting like we fresh off slavery,

and not one thing has changed!

Why not work on dual citizenship

or Garvey's back to Africa campaign?

"Because if we were still on the plantation,

You'd be the first one trying to claim,

'Massa, she should be in the field, and I should be in the house.'

Fanning the flames of resentment, without a bucket to douse.

"Jealousy... JEALOUSY

is what brings the most division and pain.

Like Cane and Abel,

it can make the best of brothers go insane.

"It's similar to 'black-on-black' crime of the Sudan,

or the 'white-on-white' crime of the Jewish holocaust.

When money and power are in the wrong hands, you see greed.

It means women, our leaders… are lost.

"Classification by race was created in 1735

by a Swedish man with a complex.

Because other than albinos, his creed was vanishing

with intermingling and sex.

And when interracial couples create more of his idea of 'blacks,'

you want to bring vex?

"But you're the main one sweating Mariah Carey and Halle Berry.

Like we're mixing donkeys with monkeys, like Harry.

"You see my husband is my yin and I am his yang.

While you may think it's strange,

balance we claim.

"I hope next time you'll change your strategy and get a clue.

I don't have to be anti-white to love myself.

And I can still be pro-black when graced by a true Afrikan king."

He said, "I am--"

I said, "a **true**."

"Because focusing on hair texture, skin color, and a last name,
Will not tell you if a cultural heritage or legacy is being maintained.

"But I'll answer that initial question: 'What are you?'
I'm Human.
And what some call His English,
a mixture of Puerto Rican, black, Cherokee, and Jew."

Do you know he simply rolled his eyes and walked away?
But I know the bright sun will shine light
on the seed I planted that day.

All blood bleeds red between him and I, and between you and me.
And as it's written in the book of Acts,
'Every nation is made of one blood.'
God shows no partiality.

So being of sound mind, I release all thoughts of racial supremacy.
Divide by flesh and be conquered, or
Unite in the Holy Spirit and live free.
And in the prophecy made most popular by Robert Nesta Marley,
"Until a man's skin is of no more significance than the color of his eyes,
War is all you will see."

Inner Peace.

FREEDOM OF CHOICE

You will never experience!

You will never understand!

You will stop trying to control my body

in the courts of this land!

Even if you changed your sex,

you can't produce what I can.

And, as a man, you can't feel what goes on inside of me.

Even another female only comprehends to a degree.

Before you dismiss the details in my case,

Look into the eyes on my face.

Sir, your life will never be on the line.

I laugh when you tell me choice is not mine!

I FOLLOW CHRIST

Jesus, what do You think
of these religious types?
I love and respect You,
but I don't believe the hype.

I don't think You want me
looking outside myself.
I'm to love the God within.
Then, somebody else.

Yet I think I could've found a humane
or sacred way without You.
But I'm glad You exist, because calling
Your name gets me through.

But I don't like saying I'm a Christian,
given Your name is used in vain.
Too many claim to be "Christ-like,"
casting judgment; placing blame.

Can you be Christian and only believe
in the words of the Messiah or Christ?
I mean shouldn't words by You,
the begotten, be enough to suffice?

Because the *Bible* and it's diverse interpretations
got folks really confused.
They're all running around looking for prosperity
and breaking all Your rules.

Very few redeliver Your Sermon on the Mount
during Sunday service.
I can see why: It makes some
of the best prophets nervous.

We're to be "perfect" just like You,
but wouldn't that make us divine?
My biggest sin: Cursing!
Lawd, You know I don't wanna give up,
flipping folks off with a sign?

But You want me to say, "yea, yea, or nay, nay,"
and simply bless all those that curse me.
I've been doing that, but can't a girl have some fun?
Must I really suffer like Thee?

You already carried the cross,

so I guess I'll take worry to the closet and pray.

"Satan, the Lord rebuke you, in Jesus name!"

I'm going to have some fun today!

So teach me, Father, how to redirect the Devil,

before he even plans an attack.

How to walk like a Goddess, following You,

knowing You always got my back!

STRANGE

So they call me strange.
Quirky.
A Weird Sistah.
Why?

Well, I feel like I'm bi,
every blue moon
if a Goddess catches my eye.

But I'm quite happy
in a monogamous or open marriage
to a straight white man
with no dream of a baby carriage!

And to some,
that makes me 'un-cool' like that.

They call me strange.
Some call me whack.

Here's the skinny:

Never had a big fatback.

Never wanted to slack.

Never wanted to be a gangsta with a gat.

Wanted to greet you with a smile and a kiss.

Never wanted to wear a poker face.

Wanted you to know, it was you that I missed.

So they call me strange.

Quirky.

A Weird Sistah.

Why?

My free spirit will never die.

My soul is as ancient as Osiris.

I see through a third eye.

But I'm still a little common,

with a pinch of style and a cup of class.

And if you give me something fried,

I'll most likely say, "Pass."

Yet I get down with "trailer trash."

And "clean camps" that roll on cash.

I'm sorry if I forgot your name,

On my mind it may not last.

I'm a poster child for raw energy,

Three letters that spell out ADD.

So I may seem a little slow,

but I'm faster than the melancholy.

So they call me strange.

Quirky.

A Weird Sistah.

Why?

I get high off natural air.

My personality will come in a pair.

Gemini coasters, wanna go for a ride?

Checking myself daily,

cause I'm packing a whole lot of pride.

Rolling solo by choice.

Made friends with that inner voice.

Evolving for the calling,

still, you'll find me stalling.

But you'll never catch me locking the door.

I let the most high keep spiritual score.

I know it's easier to blend and

often I see us as the same.

But I accept that I am different,

as my fingerprint and middle name.

So if you're feeing like an outsider

and maybe you've been labeled, too.

I have one quote that might help:

"To thine own self, be true!"

OCCUPATION WALL STREET (O.W.S.)

Oh say can you see,

beyond race, sex, and nationality?

Forget orientation,

because your class is in session in the streets.

Will you attend?

Do you have an occupation this week?

"Get a job!" he yells to all those on the corner in protest.

"There are no jobs!" they chant, to an unresponsive Congress.

Hallowed be thy names,

all those homeless in pain.

Because white collars and blue collars are not the same.

Main Street was shut down,

but Wall Street is too big to fail!

Equivalency is heavenly,

but if you're in the wrong class, it's hell!

UNEQUAL CLASSES

There are far too many children being left behind.

We invest in jails more than schools. What a crime!

Bobby works, cooks, and cleans for his sick mother at night.

Her heart medicine costs Franklins, and money is tight.

I'm glad he has a neighbor who looks after him with care.

Every child forced to work knows that life isn't fair.

"What class is he in?" Do I really need to ask?

So poor, he drops out and no one holds him to task!

Most public schools really need Uncle Sam.

Where students can barely read, *Sam-I-Am*.

Are those teachers the ones they refuse to inspect?

Unmotivated with tenure, looking for a check!

If Bobby were your son, what would you do?

The classes he's in affect everything, it's true.

The masses must move, but it must be the classes that move them.

We replant for growth, when the house is condemned.

The masses must move, but it must be the classes that move them.

We're scrambling, through a pile of rocks for one desired gem.

We know it's a system established in the past.

What will we instill and how long will it last?

Because, educate a few; low standards for the rest.

Or survival of the fittest isn't working at best!

So do we want critical thinkers who seek to progress?

Is it wise to have citizens who question Congress?

We want solutions that move the masses,

but we are still living in unequal classes.

Ignorance means ignoring history's lessons again.

We're bound to study when we want imperialism to end.

The masses must move, but it must be the classes that move them.

We focus on the root, not the leaf or the stem.

The masses must move, but it must be the classes that move them.

We replant for growth, when the house is condemned.

EDUCATED GIRL

I got a degree now.
Running a book store
on the west side of town.
Business isn't any good though.
Very little money around.

Degrees are just accomplishments,
like everything else, I guess.
Maybe a little luck now?
Maybe I can get a fancy dress?

Show up and show out, girl!
Maybe some good help soon.
Good help is hard to find,
but two customers come to swoon.

Maybe no luck for a long time.
Only bills on the up-and-up.
I've got blues and blessings
to count in my rusty tin cup.

Wish everyone read real books.
That would be really cool!
I've been running this business too long.
Guess I'll go back to school.

LYRICS FOR LANGSTON

You were born in Missouri,
raised in Cleveland.
That sounds a lot like me!
You attended Central High,
and I attended McKinley.

I too remember being in a packed house,
pondering plays at Karamu.
Langston, I feel we have a connection,
so what's a girl to do?

I'm usually not this forward,
but you had me at "deferred."
Now all of my dreams look like
Coltrane's, Duke's, Monk's, or Byrd's.

"To be loved by you"
is the song I sing.
"How sweet it is!" I shout!
I can conjure spirits,
but I've come to think.
You're my main muse,
without a doubt!

Epilogue

LANGSTON HUGHES

James Langston Hughes
was born on February 1, 1902, in
Joplin, Missouri. His parents
divorced when he was a small child
and his father moved to Mexico. His
grandmother raised him until he was
thirteen, when he moved to Lincoln,
Illinois to live with his mother and
her husband. The family eventually
settled in Cleveland, Ohio.

It was in Illinois that Hughes began writing poetry. Following graduation,
he spent a year in Mexico and a year at Columbia University. During
these years, he held odd jobs as an assistant cook, launderer, and a
busboy, and traveled to Africa and Europe working as a seaman. In
November 1924, he moved to Washington, D.C.

Hughes's first book of poetry, *The Weary Blues*, was published by Alfred A.
Knopf in 1926. He finished his college education at Lincoln University in
Pennsylvania three years later. In 1930 his first novel, *Not Without
Laughter*, won the Harmon gold medal for literature. He was known for
his engagement with the world of jazz and the influence it had on his
writing, as in *Montage of a Dream Deferred*.

His life and work were enormously important in shaping the artistic contributions of the Harlem Renaissance of the 1920s. Hughes refused to differentiate between his personal experience and the common experience of black America. He wanted to tell the stories of his people in ways that reflected their actual culture, including both their suffering and their love of music, laughter, and language itself.

In his memory, his residence at 20 East 127th Street in Harlem has been given landmark status by the New York City Preservation Commission, and East 127th Street has been renamed "Langston Hughes Place."

VENUS JONES

Venus Jones was born June 5, 1974 in Kansas City, Missouri. Her biological mother became ill and gave her away to a woman she trusted at her nearby church. When Venus was the tender age of two, she moved with her new mother to Ohio.

It was in Akron where she began writing poetry in her diary. Following graduation, she spent a summer in Washington D.C, then earned a B.A. in Communications at The University of Akron. She was awarded best on-air personality at the local radio station and landed an internship as one of the first local correspondents for MTV Online. During her undergraduate studies of broadcasting and business, she was also heavily involved in theatre and appeared in plays at Weathervane Theatre. Meanwhile she was the chair of the cultural diversity committee, where she produced educational and entertaining programming for the campus.

In July 1998, she moved to Tampa, Florida. She began working backstage at The Home Shopping Network, and later became an accomplished commercial model and voice-over artist with hundreds of commercials to her credit. In 2002, she was asked to be the resident poet

Art as Activism

Readers and audiences everywhere are RAVING about

She Rose

your journey from girl to Goddess

e Rose is a keynote presentation that includes a personal narrative, poetry, ought provoking quotes and tributes to female heroes of the past and present.

Learn how to:

- **Embrace** the light or god/dess within and rise to your fullest potential
- **Engage** in healthier conversations by asking quality questions
- **Share** a story that promotes equity and equality
- **Lead** like a Hero or Shero who made a difference in your life

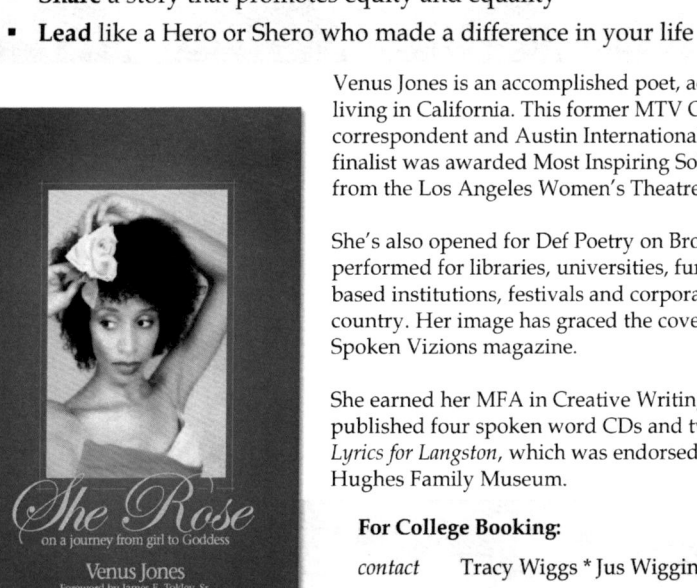

Venus Jones is an accomplished poet, actress, and educator living in California. This former MTV Online correspondent and Austin International Poetry Slam finalist was awarded Most Inspiring Solo Performance from the Los Angeles Women's Theatre Festival in 2012.

She's also opened for Def Poetry on Broadway and performed for libraries, universities, fundraisers, faith based institutions, festivals and corporations across the country. Her image has graced the cover of billboards and Spoken Vizions magazine.

She earned her MFA in Creative Writing and has published four spoken word CDs and two books including *Lyrics for Langston*, which was endorsed by the Langston Hughes Family Museum.

For College Booking:

contact   Tracy Wiggs * Jus Wiggin Entertainment

email   juswign@yahoo.com

phone   (301)221-4540

of the WMNF talk show "The Sunday Forum." She moved on to record her first poetry CD, entitled "Venus to Earth," and famed poet Nikki Giovanni endorsed her first book, *She Rose: On a Journey from girl to Goddess.* She opened for Def Poetry on Broadway, and her work has appeared in *Poet Lore*, UK's *X Magazine*, *Spoken Vizions* magazine, and anthologies including, "How I Freed My Soul", "A Time to Rhyme" and "A Generation Defining Itself."

In May 2014, she earned her M.F.A. in Poetry and Creative Writing from Mills College in Oakland, California. She continues to serve her community as a youth facilitator and program developer for many in school and after school programs.

The rest is Her Story in the making.

Made in the USA
San Bernardino, CA
01 November 2016